CUBE
BOOK

WONDERS OF
ITALY

WHITE STAR PUBLISHERS

text
GABRIELE ATRIPALDI

graphic design
CLARA ZANOTTI

graphic layout
MARIA CUCCHI

translation
ALAN GOLDWATER

editorial coordination
LAURA ACCOMAZZO
VALENTINA GIAMMARINARO

© 2010 **EDIZIONI WHITE STAR S.R.L.**
VIA CANDIDO SASSONE, 24
13100 VERCELLI - ITALY
WWW.WHITESTAR.IT

● Mist enveloping the hills around Siena.

ISBN 978-88-544-0545-5

1 2 3 4 5 6 14 13 12 11 10

Printed in Indonesia

CONTENTS

WONDERS OF ITALY

1 • Piazza del Duomo in Pisa, where we find the Cathedral, the Battistero, Campo Santo as well as the world famous Leaning Tower.

2-3 • The Spiaggia dei Conigli (Rabbit Beach) is an offshoot of the Island of Lampedusa.

4-5 • Grandes Jorasses, in the Mont Blanc Massif, are the most majestic and picturesque peaks in Valle d'Aosta.

6-7 • Santa Maria della Salute is one of Venice's best examples of Baroque architecture.

8-9 • The Roman forum, in the heart of the city, comprises a series of monumental squares built over the centuries.

13 • Etna is one of the myriad natural wonders of Sicily.

14-15 • Thun Castle stands on the summit of a hill overlooking the town of Ton, in Val di Non.

16-17 • Florence undoubtedly is still one of the preeminent wonders of the Bel Paese.

18-19 • The volcanic Island of Capraia, characterized by its high, rocky, coastline.

Introduction

ITALY IS LIKE A BOX OF PRECIOUS JEWELS BRIMMING WITH SCENIC, ARCHAEOLOGICAL AND ARTISTIC WONDERS SET AGAINST A BACKGROUND OF ANCIENT TRADITIONS AND FOLKLORE. THIS COUNTRY HAS PRODUCED ENLIGHTENED MINDS WHO HAVE PERMANENTLY ALTERED THE COURSE OF HUMAN HISTORY, FROM LEONARDO DA VINCI TO MARCONI, VOLTA, FERMI MEUCCI AND INNUMERABLE OTHERS, ALONG WITH EXTRAORDINARY TALENTS WHO HAVE CONTRIBUTED SO MUCH TO THE WORLD OF ART. ITALIAN GENIUS IS SO SUCCESSFUL IN THE WORLDS OF FASHION, DESIGN, AND JEWELRY, THAT THE MOTTO "MADE IN ITALY" IS NOW A SYNONYM FOR UNRIVALED STYLE AND GOOD

Orvieto Cathedral is one of the masterpieces of central Italian Gothic architecture.

Introduction

TASTE. ITALY IS A HOTBED OF CREATIVE FERMENT: ITS WORKMANSHIP TOUCHES HEIGHTS OF PROVERBIAL MASTERY AND GARNERS UNIVERSAL ADMIRATION, WHILE ITS CINEMA IS INTERNATIONALLY RENOWNED THANKS TO FELLINI, ZEFFIRELLI, DE LAURENTIIS, LOREN, LOLLOBRIGIDA, MAGNANI, AND OSCAR WINNER BENIGNI. ITALY, MORE THAN MOST COUNTRIES, NOW REPRESENTS A UNIQUE BRAND NAME. THIS REPUTATION IS OF COURSE ALWAYS ENHANCED BY ITS COLORFUL AND VARIED FOOD AND DRINK (IT IS, AFTER ALL, THE HOME OF THE MEDITERRANEAN DIET, SPAGHETTI AND MOZZARELLA), BY THE GREAT SENSE OF HOSPITALITY OF ITS PEOPLE AND BY ITS SUCCESS AT SOCCER. SOME OF THIS APPRECIATION IS ALSO DUE TO THE SACRIFICES OF

Introduction

GENERATIONS OF EMIGRANTS WHO HAVE HELPED KEEP THE *TRICOLORE* FLAG FLYING IN EVERY CORNER OF THE WORLD.

WHILE NOT DENYING THE EXISTENCE OF A NUMBER OF PROBLEMS AND ENDEMIC CONTRADICTIONS, ITALY'S MAIN CHALLENGE TODAY IS TO MAKE THIS VAST WEALTH OF BEAUTY, CULTURE, TASTE, AND FRIENDLINESS MORE ACCESSIBLE TO EVERYONE.

TRAVELING THROUGH THIS PECULIARLY BOOT-SHAPED LAND SET IN THE CENTER OF THE MEDITERRANEAN BASIN, A CROSSROADS BETWEEN EUROPE, AFRICA AND ASIA, WE CAN FULLY APPRECIATE ITS BEWITCHING APPEAL: FROM THE ALPS, THE MOUNTAIN RANGE THAT MAJESTICALLY CROWNS THE FAR NORTH AND SEPA-

Introduction

RATES THE PENINSULA FROM THE REST OF CONTINEN-
TAL EUROPE, TO THE PICTURESQUE APENNINE CHAIN,
THE SPINE OF ITALY THAT STRETCHES FOR MORE THAN
A THOUSAND KILOMETERS CREATING THE CLIMATIC
VARIATIONS THAT MOULD THE LANDSCAPE, ALL THE
WAY DOWN TO THE CITRUS FIELDS AND LIGHT OF A
TROUBLED BUT INDOMITABLE SOUTH. ITALY'S RIVERS
ARE SHORTER THAN THE AVERAGE FOR EUROPE BUT
NOT LACKING IN NUMBER. THERE ARE MANY ENCHANT-
ING LAKES, MOST OF WHICH ARE IN THE NORTH OR
CENTRE. THE COUNTRY'S STUNNING COASTS ARE
RENOWNED WORLDWIDE, AND ALONG WITH THE IS-
LANDS ARE OFTEN EXCLUSIVE TOURIST DESTINATIONS.
ENCHANTING HAMLETS, TOWNS AND CITIES, BIG AND

Introduction

SMALL, IN WHICH MILLENNIA OF HISTORY COEXIST WITH A DETERMINATION TO LOOK TO THE FUTURE COUNT AMONG ITS MOST PRECIOUS GEMS: RANGING FROM THE INDUSTRIOUS AND QUINTESSENTIALLY EUROPEAN MILAN, TO ROMANTIC VENICE WITH ITS LOVELY ATMOSPHERIC LAGOONS, TO THE FLORENCE OF DANTE, BRUNELLESCHI, BENVENUTO CELLINI AND BOTTICELLI, TO ROME *CAPUT MUNDI*, TO THE NAPLES OF VESUVIUS, PIZZA, AND THE PALAZZO REALE, AND TO PALERMO, WITH ITS ARCHITECTURAL TRACES OF DOMINATION BY ROMANS, BYZANTINES, ARABS AND NORMANS, ALL MAGICALLY ENTWINED, ITALY REALLY IS LIKE A JEWEL CASE PACKED WITH PRICELESS AND UNIQUE TREASURES.

Introduction

THIS VOLUME USES PICTURES OF A LAND ENRICHED BY ITS SPECTACULAR AND VARIED NATURE, OFFERING THE READER THE KEY TO OPEN THAT JEWEL CASE AND TO DISCOVER (OR REDISCOVER) THE *BEL PAESE* WITH ALL ITS INCOMPARABLE WONDERS.

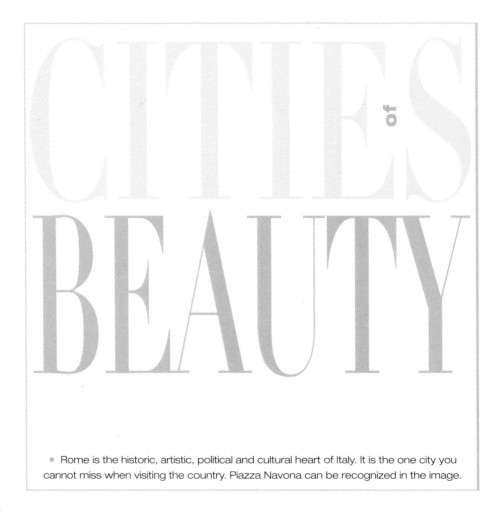

CITIES of BEAUTY

- Rome is the historic, artistic, political and cultural heart of Italy. It is the one city you cannot miss when visiting the country. Piazza Navona can be recognized in the image.

INTRODUCTION Cities of beauty

If we agree with Calvino, who wrote, "You do not gain from the seven or seventy-seven wonders of a city, but from the answer it gives to one of your questions," (Italo Calvino, *Invisible Cities*, Turin, Einaudi, 1972), then perhaps Italy's cities use wonder as their main tool for answering our questions: all of them. And if the answers we seek concern life, beauty, and love, it won't be hard to find them in our amazement at the residents of the Genoa Aquarium, or in the breathtaking frescos of the cupola of the Duomo of Florence. Indeed, nor will it be difficult to glimpse these answers among those watery reflections that lap against languid Venetian gondolas. Italy's main

An aerial view of Ragusa (Sicily), containing some of the most important architecture and art of the Baroque.

INTRODUCTION Cities of beauty

TOWNS AND CITIES ABOUND WITH SQUARES THAT OOZE HISTORY (LIKE PIAZZA UNITÀ D'ITALIA, WHICH OVERLOOKS THE GULF OF TRIESTE) AND CHURCHES (LIKE SANTA MARIA DELLE GRAZIE THAT HOUSES LEONARDO DA VINCI'S LAST SUPPER). THERE ARE CAFES WHERE POETS, ARTISTS AND WRITERS USED TO MEET AND MAJOR LIBRARIES THAT GUARD THE SECRETS OF THE NATIONAL LIBRARY (AMONG WHICH ARE THE NATIONAL BRAIDENSE LIBRARY AND THE PINACOTECA LIBRARY OF THE AMBROSIAN ACADEMY LIBRARY). THERE ARE ALSO SHOP WINDOWS DISPLAYING THE ITALY'S FAMOUS STYLE, ALONG WEALTHY STREETS SYNONYMOUS WITH FASHION, LIKE VIA CONDOTTI IN ROME OR VIA MONTENAPOLEONE IN MILAN. THE RESTAURANTS OFFER HEAVENLY DISHES AND ITS THEATERS VENUES FOR ACTORS TO WRESTLE WITH PLAYS

INTRODUCTION Cities of beauty

RANGING FROM THE CLASSICAL TO THE AVANT-GARDE. THEN THE SAN CARLO IN NAPLES, THE REOPENED PETRUZZELLI IN BARI, IN MILAN'S LA SCALA AND MANY OTHERS, ARE TEMPLES FOR THE ETERNAL MUSIC OF VERDI, ROSSINI, DONIZETTI, MASCAGNI, AND PUCCINI, PERFORMED BY ORCHESTRAS AND BY THE VOICES OF FROM RENATA TEBALDI TO GIUSEPPE DI STEFANO TO CARUSO TO BENIAMINO GIGLI TO PAVAROTTI AND BOCELLI. THROUGHOUT THE ENTIRE PENINSULAR, HUMAN EN-DEAVOR, EXPRESSED OVER THE COURSE OF CENTURIES, HAS GIVEN RISE TO MONUMENTS, CATHEDRALS AND CASTLES: FROM THE ARISTOCRATIC MANTUA, AN EXTRAORDINARILY BEAUTIFUL RENAISSANCE TOWN PACKED FULL OF SQUARES, TOWERS AND HISTORIC BUILDINGS, TO CREMONA, CITY OF THE DUOMO THAT SITS ALONGSIDE THE LOFTY TORRAZZO

Cities of beauty

Introduction

WHERE A MASTER LUTHIER, STRADIVARIUS, CREATED THE MOST PRECIOUS VIOLINS IN THE WORLD; TO PARMA, GASTRONOMIC PARADISE AND AT THE SAME TIME THE HOME OF INCREDIBLE ART; TO PISA, WHOSE PIAZZA DEI MIRACOLI IS FAMOUS FOR THE CAMPANILE, THE LEANING BELL TOWER THAT HAS BECOME AN ICON THE WORLD OVER; TO ORVIETO, WHOSE DUOMO IS ONE OF THE MOST SPECTACULAR CATHEDRALS IN ITALY; TO POZZUOLI, WITH ITS TWO ROMAN AMPHITHEATERS; TO MATERA, THE CENTER OF WHICH IS FAMOUS FOR ITS SASSI (NEIGHBORHOODS CARVED OUT OF ROCK); TO TAORMINA, WHERE IT IS IMPOSSIBLE TO RESISTS THE CHARM OF THE GREEK THEATER. ITALY'S CITIES DON'T SPEAK, BUT THEY KNOW HOW TO ANSWER OUR MOST INTIMATE QUESTIONS.

- Milan is an extraordinarily lively city. The teeming city center is full of busy passersby, there either to work or shop. The photograph shows the Galleria Vittorio Emanuele II.

44 • The statue of Emanuel Philibert on horseback putting his sword away after the battle of San Quintino holds pride of place in the center of Piazza San Carlo, one of Turin's main squares.

45 • The extremely high Mole Antonelliana, 549,5 ft (167.5 m), is the symbol of Turin. Its spire overlooks the city and seems to soar upwards to the clouds.

46 • The Palazzina di Caccia of Stupinigi, in the midst of a lovely park,
is home to the Museo di Arte e Ammobiliamento.

47 • The crypt of the Basilica of Superga, situated in the town of the same name
in the Province of Turin, hosts the Royal Tombs of the House of Savoy.

48 ● The Basilica of Sant'Andrea in Vercelli is renowned for an elegance that can be seen in the sober colors of its façade.

49 ● Again in Vercelli, Cavour's statue stands in the center of Piazza Cavour, with the Torre dell'Angelo in the background.

Alessandria's unusual star-shaped eighteenth century military Citadel is of great visual and architectural interest.

52 • Piazza Martiri della Libertà in the heart of the city of Novara, is home to the Castello Sforzesco (Sforza Castle), the Palazzo del Mercato and the Teatro Coccia.

53 • An aerial view of the roofs of the city of Novara, prominent among which are the cupola and bell tower of the Basilica of San Gaudenzio.

54-55 • A wonderful picture of Lake Como, with the Tempio Voltiano (on the left of the photograph) and the Villa Olmo (bottom right).

56 • The town of Como on the Swiss border is at the southernmost point of the western bank of the Lake Como. The photograph shows the zone known as Lungo Lario Trento.

57 • The Lombard city of Como is packed full of extraordinary art, culture and architecture. The splendid Duomo, with its Latin cross shaped layout, is just one example of this.

58-59 ● The picturesque Ponte Vecchio in Pavia, on the Ticino river, connects the Borgo Ticino district with the town center.

59 ● The University of Pavia was founded by the Emperor Lotharius in AD 825, and has been renowned for its brilliant law school since the Middle Ages.

The Certosa di Pavia monastery is an extraordinary architectural complex, whose construction began at the end of the fourteenth century on the initiative of Gian Galeazzo Visconti.

62 • The historical symbol of Milan, the Duomo is an inimitable and fundamental example of Gothic architecture.

62-63 • The Milan Duomo provides the background to the statue of Vittorio Emanuele II, in the center of Piazza del Duomo.

A picturesque view of Castello Sforzesco in the Lombard capital, damaged and renovated on a number of occasions over the centuries.

66-67 • The Naviglio Grande is a piece of medieval engineering initially conceived as an irrigation channel and subsequently used for trade and transport.

68-69 • An aerial view of Mantua, which under the Gonzagas was a center of artistic production admired the world over.

70-71 • Palazzo Pretorio, in Piazza del Duomo in Trento, is the background to the Fountain of Neptune, adorned with various groups of sculptures.

71 • The small Eagle Fountain, in Trento's provincial capital, depicts a bird of prey resting on a lime column.

72 • The Verona Arena, along with the house of Juliet, is the international symbol of this city.

72-73 • Verona, whose city center has been declared a UNESCO World Heritage Site, receives huge numbers of tourists every year.

74-75 • Padua's monumental Basilica of Saint Anthony is the city's most important sacred place.

75 • The enormous Prato della Valle, in Padua, is one of the largest squares in Europe. Its elliptically shaped central island is surrounded by two rows of statues separated by a small canal.

Its extraordinary geographical location makes "The Most Serene Republic of Venice," as it used to be called, a place of unrivalled beauty.

78 • St Mark's Square in Venice is instantly recognizable the world over, the eternal symbol of that city.

79 • The majestic St Mark's Basilica houses an infinite variety of masterpieces of various provenance, collected by the Venetians over the centuries.

80 • The Rialto Bridge is one of the most romantic points in Venice, known the world over for its quintessentially Venetian atmosphere.

81 • These staffs are typical moorings used in the Venice lagoon.

Every corner of Trieste is a marvel and the panoramic Miramare Castle, surrounded by an extraordinary park housing the important Historical Museum, is its hub.

LLOYD TRIESTINO

84-85 ● Trieste's Palazzo Gopcevich, with its original frescoes, houses the Carlo Schmidl Theatre Museum.

85 ● The cupola of the Church of San Spiridione is the magnificent place of worship of Trieste's Serbian Orthodox community.

The mild climate of Sanremo, "City of Flowers," famous for its Italian Song Festival and Casino, makes it a year round tourist destination.

88 ● This former private residence of Prince Andrea Doria, in Genoa, was built in the sixteenth century. It is surrounded by a splendid Italian-style garden with a Fountain of Neptune.

88-89 ● Genoa's majestic Palazzo Reale is one of the city's historical buildings recently declared a UNESCO World Heritage Site.

90-91 and 91 • At left, the amazing Genoa Aquarium. On the right the famous Lantern, the historic lighthouse that has become the symbol of Genoa.

92-93 • The former Piazza Grande in Piacenza (Emilia Romagna) is today called Piazza dei Cavalli (Horses' Square) due to the lovely equestrian statues in front of the city hall.

94 • The center of Reggio Emilia is home to the Civic Theatre, the Duomo and the Basilicas of the Beata Vergine della Ghiara and San Prospero.

94-95 • Modena is a jewel of inestimable value. Its Torre Civica, Cathedral and Piazza Grande are UNESCO World Heritage Sites.

96 ● A view of Bologna, in which the two famous medieval towers (of Asinelli and Garisenda) stand out.

96-97 ● Piazza Maggiore, the heart of Bologna, is the site of a number of historic buildings, including Palazzo dei Notai and Palazzo d'Accursio.

● When visiting Ferrara
you must visit Castello
Estense, built in the
fourteenth century but
altered and renovated a
number of times down
the centuries.

The medieval Piazza del Duomo is Parma's pride and joy. It contains the Palazzo Episcopale (Bishop's Palace), the Battistero and the magnificent Cathedral.

102-103 ● Lucca's splendid Piazza dell'Anfiteatro is elliptical in shape because it was built on the remains of an ancient Roman theatre.

103 ● The statue of Francesco Burlamacchi was placed in the center of Lucca's Piazza San Michele in 1863.

Piazza dei Miracoli in Pisa is a concentrate of history, extraordinary architecture and irresistible charm, a perennial attraction for tourists from all around the world.

106-107 •
Brunelleschi's
extraordinary cupola
distinguishes Florence's
Cathedral of Santa
Maria del Fiore.

108-109 •
A picturesque shot of
Ponte Vecchio, a bridge
over Florence's River
Arno. There are many
goldsmiths' workshops
in the surrounding area.

110 • The beauty of Palazzo Vecchio outshines everything else in Florence's Piazza della Signoria. A copy of Michelangelo's David stands in front.

111 • An aerial view of the center of Florence. We can make out Piazza della Signoria and the Uffizi Gallery.

● Siena's Santa Maria Assunta Cathedral
overlooks the city. The marble work floor
is outstanding.

114-115 ● Urbino, a lovely city set amongst wonderful hills, gave birth to the famous Renaissance painter Raphael, amongst others.

116-117 ● Perugia, regional capital of Umbria, is packed with historical, artistic, architectural and archaeological marvels. It is a real cultural paradise.

118 and 119 • Assisi was the birthplace of Saint Clare, founder of the monastic Order of Poor Ladies, and of Saint Francis, patron saint of Italy.

120-121 • The magnificent Umbrian town of Orvieto is built on an enormous tufa rock (known as 'The Cliff'), and dominates the surrounding countryside.

• The eighteenth century Trevi Fountain in Rome was the location for a famous scene from *La Dolce Vita*, by Federico Fellini.

124-125 • A picture of the Capitoline, home to Rome's city hall. In the center, we see a copy of an ancient equestrian statue of Marcus Aurelius.

125 • The column dedicated to the Roman emperor Marcus Aurelius, outside the Alberto Sordi Gallery (formerly Palazzo della Galleria Colonna).

Castel Sant'Angelo, on the bank of the Tiber, is the mausoleum of the Emperor Hadrian (from which comes the name Hadrian's Mole).

An aerial view of Piazza Venezia in Rome and the Vittoriano complex, the national monument dedicated to Vittorio Emanuele II of Savoy, the first King of Italy.

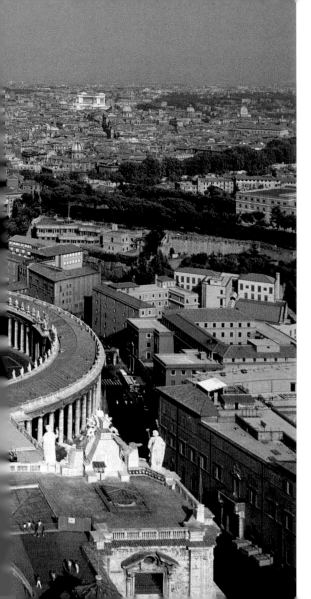

- St Peter's Square is the heart of
  the Vatican. Every Sunday the
  Pope addresses thousands of
  Roman Catholics who come
  for his blessing.

132-133 • St Peter's Basilica is the architectural and spiritual heart of St Peter's Square, as well as one of the grandest places of worship in the world.

133 • A visit to the interior of St Peter's Basilica is an unforgettable experience. We come face to face with extraordinary works of art, like the monumental Baldachin created by Bernini in the seventeenth century.

A stunning picture of the city of Rome at sunset. As the Tiber placidly follows its course, the cupola of St Peter's seems to watch over the city.

136 • Piazza del Plebiscito is the main square in Naples, in which we find the famous Church of San Francesco di Paola.

136-137 • Mergellina faces the sea. It's one of the most picturesque parts of the splendid city of Naples.

Built at the end of the nineteenth century, the picturesque Galleria Umberto I
is one of delights of the city of Naples.

Castel dell'Ovo, built on a small island of tufa, is one of the most prestigious and important historical buildings in Naples.

142-143 ● An aerial view of the Royal Palace of Caserta, the majestic former residence of the Bourbons and now a UNESCO World Heritage Site.

143 ● A magnificent park surrounds the Royal Palace of Caserta.

144-145 ● The unusual layout of Matera's neighborhoods (the Sassi) has made the city famous worldwide, so much so that it is a UNESCO World Heritage Site.

146 • Bari's Petruzzeli Theatre was carefully restored to its original splendor in every detail after the fire of 1991.

147 • The Romanesque church of St Nicholas, patron saint of Bari, is in the city center.

148 ● Taranto is a pearl. It looks out over a blue sea and is Italy's second biggest port.

148-149 ● The Basilica of Santa Croce, in Lecce, is one of the most important and attractive architectural complexes in the beautiful Apulian city.

The town of Gallipoli, in the Province of Lecce, faces the Ionian Sea. The town center is on an island connected to the mainland by an eighteenth century bridge.

● Otranto is Italy's easternmost city and looks out over an extraordinarily beautiful sea.

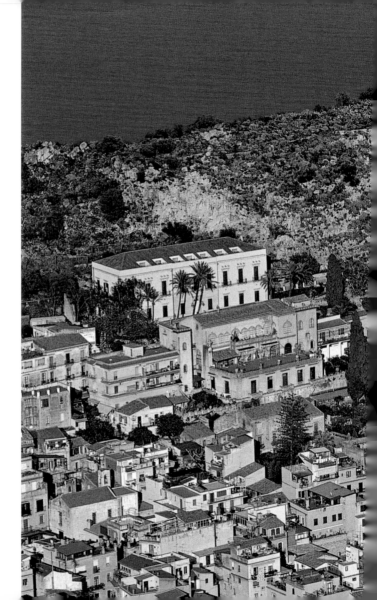

 A picturesque view of the tourist resort of Taormina, as seen from its splendid Greek Theatre.

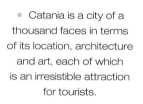 Catania is a city of a thousand faces in terms of its location, architecture and art, each of which is an irresistible attraction for tourists.

Palermo Cathedral is the result
of a surprising combination
of architectural styles.

160 ● The Cathedral of Santa Maria di Castello, in Cagliari, Sardinia, is the harmonious result of a blend of different architectural styles.

160-161 ● The regional capital, Cagliari, looks out over Sardinia's extraordinary sea. The city is divided into 33 districts.

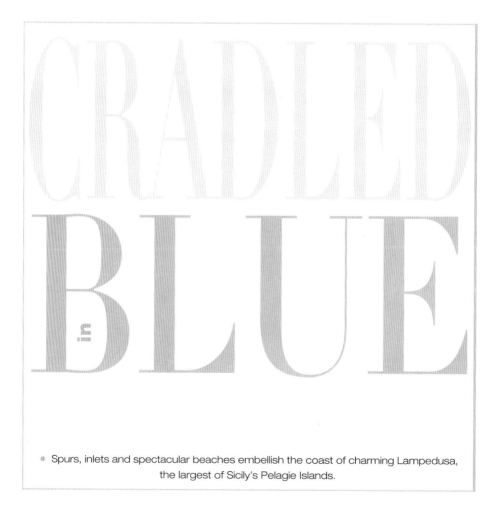

CRADLED IN BLUE

Spurs, inlets and spectacular beaches embellish the coast of charming Lampedusa, the largest of Sicily's Pelagie Islands.

INTRODUCTION Cradled in blue

From rocky and foreboding cliffs with crashing waves beneath, to clear, calm aquamarine waters, the shores of the Italian peninsula are as varied as they are breathtaking.

The Ligurian Riviera extends in an arc along the sea of the same name and is the natural outlet for many northern regions. Genoa divides it into two strips: the Levante Riviera (from the Tuscan border) and the Ponente Riviera (up to the French border). The former, jagged and full of lovely rocky peaks jutting out over the sea, includes the Paradise Gulf, a jewel of uncontaminated beauty, the Tigullio, the Baia delle Favole (Bay of Fables) and the Baia del

• The picturesque village of San Rocco looks out over the Gulf of Tigullio from Portofino Promontory.

INTRODUCTION Cradled in blue

SILENZIO (BAY OF SILENCE), CINQUE TERRE, A UNESCO WORLD HERITAGE SITE, AND THE GULF OF LA SPEZIA, ALSO KNOWN AS THE GULF OF THE POETS. THE TYRRHENIAN LAPS AGAINST THE LONGEST STRETCH OF TUSCAN COAST (OPPOSITE THE GLITTERING ISLAND JEWELS OF ELBA, GIANNUTRI AND GIGLIO).

THEN THE LAZIO COAST (WITH THE VAST GULF OF GAETA LOOKING OUT TO THE PONTINE ISLANDS) IS PACKED WITH THE LUXURY YACHTS OF THE INTERNATIONAL JET SET. HEADING SOUTH WE COME TO THE COAST OF CAMPANIA (PROCIDA, ISCHIA AND CAPRI STAND OUT IN THE GULF OF NAPLES, KNOWN WORLDWIDE FOR THEIR AMAZING SEA STACKS) AND THEN THE CALABRIAN COAST, FIRST IRREGULAR AND THEN RECTILINEAR, BUT ALWAYS BATHED BY A

INTRODUCTION Cradled in blue

COBALT BLUE SEA OF ALMOST UNREAL BEAUTY. THE IONIAN RIVIERA HAS THE WIND-BEATEN GULF OF SQUILLACE, AND THE GULF OF TARANTO OPPOSITE THE SMALL CHERADI ARCHIPELAGO. PAST OTRANTO AND UP TO RAVENNA, EXCEPT FOR THE PROMONTORIES OF GARGANO (ALONG WHICH APULIA STRETCHES OUT INTO THE ADRIATIC) AND CONERO (WHERE ANCONA IS BUILT), THE COASTS ARE LOWER, SANDY, AND UNIFORM. THE EMILIA-ROMAGNA COASTLINE IS PACKED FULL OF VENERABLE AND WELL-RUN SEASIDE RESORTS. THE FINAL STRETCH OF THE ADRIATIC COAST IS PARTICULARLY JAGGED, OVERLOOKING THE PO DELTA AND THE GULFS OF VENICE AND TRIESTE.

SICILY AND SARDINIA, THE LARGEST OF ITALY'S ISLANDS, ARE PARADISE FOR TOURISTS: THE FORMER SURROUNDED BY

Cradled in blue
Introduction

THE WONDERFUL LAMPEDUSA, PANTELLERIA, USTICA, AS WELL AS THE AEGADIAN AND AEOLIAN ISLANDS. THE LATTER IS THE LAND OF THE EMERALD SEA AND DAZZLING WHITE SAND, PACKED WITH EXCLUSIVE HOLIDAY RESORTS AND FAMOUS FOR ITS GLITTERING SUMMER NIGHTLIFE.

THE EDGES OF THE BOOT OF ITALY ARE STUDDED WITH COASTS AND ISLANDS DRAWING US TO THEM LIKE SIRENS, LAPPED AS THEY ARE BY THE LEGENDARY BEAUTY OF THE MEDITERRANEAN.

169 • Capo Bianco is the promontory of the Island of Ponza.

170-171 • Along the Ligurian coast of Cinque Terre, the Marine Protected Area and the National Park safeguard an extraordinarily varied nature.

172 • The colorful houses of Manarola, looking out over the sea, make it one of the most enchanting villages in the whole of Italy.

172-173 • Many of the steep slopes surrounding the village of Manarola have been terraced for agricultural use.

Varigotti in Liguria is known for its long sandy beach, packed with summer beach clubs.

176-177 • A shot of picturesque Cala Rossa on the Island of Capraia, whose strong coloration contrasts spectacularly with the white rock of the nearby promontory of Zenobito.

177 • A colony of seagulls has found refuge among the rocks of Capraia, pearl of the Tuscan Archipelago.

Capo Testa is a peninsula in northern Sardinia, not far from Santa Teresa di Gallura, whose crystalline waters attract tourists from around the world.

180-181 ● The jagged coast of the Island of Budelli, in the Maddalena Archipelago (Sardinia) is considered one of the most beautiful in the Mediterranean.

181 ● A spontaneous efflorescence of bright colors embellishes the sand dunes between Palau and Capo Testa, Sardinia.

182-183 ● A crystal sea laps against the rocks of an idyllic cove on the Island of Budelli.

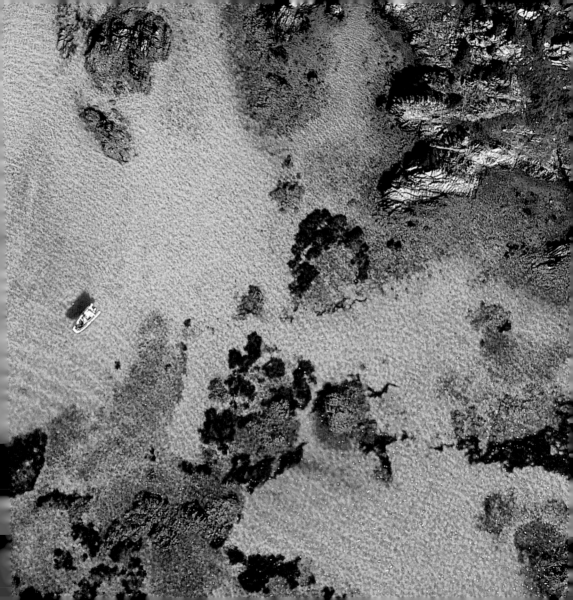

184-185 • Cala Viola, one of the lovely beaches of northwest Sardinia between Capo dell'Argentiera and the promontory of Capo Caccia.

186-187 • Capo Falcone is the most northwesterly point of Sardinia. It faces the lovely Gulf of Asinara.

188 ● Ponza is the queen of the Pontine islands. Surrounded by an extraordinary sea, it is a summer favorite of the international jet set. The picture shows Cala Inferno.

188-189 ● The beach of Chiaia di Luna, on Ponza, boasts one of the most picturesque views on the island.

190-191 and *191* ● The Amalfi Coast is a jagged coast of undisputable beauty. It became a UNESCO World Heritage Site in 1997.

192-193 ● Ravello occupies a plateau on the Amalfi Coast and enjoys a famous view of the Gulf of Salerno.

● The Aragonese
Castle of Ischia is
situated on a small
island connected by a
stone bridge to the
ancient village of Celsa,
today known as
Ischia Ponte.

196 ● Mergellina, the lively port area of Naples, is built on the slope of Posillipo hill.

196-197 ● Corricella, an ancient fishing village with an eighteenth century marina, stands out among the villages of the Island of Procida.

The Island of Vulcano, cooled by the fresh sea breezes that compensate for the lack of rain, has a surface area of just 8 sq mi (21 square kilometers).

A beautiful picture of the stacks in the sea between Lipari (from where the photograph was taken) and Vulcano (bottom).

202-203 • Alicudi, the most unusual and picturesquely shaped of the Aeolian islands, is also the most recently formed.

203 • The enchanting, uncontaminated beauty of Filicudi, also part of the Aeolian archipelago, has made it a UNESCO World Heritage Site.

The Island of Salina has the highest mountains in the Aeolian islands and was the location for *Il Postino*, the famous movie starring Masssimo Troisi.

Linosa is a wonderful volcanic island. The elegant buildings of its only town are clustered around a small marina.

208-209 • Dark volcanic rocks contrast with intense green vegetation on the island of Linosa.

209 • The steep rocky slopes of Cala Pozzolana, on the Island of Linosa, overhang the sea.

210-211 • Not far from the coast of Africa, Lampedusa is bathed by a sea of beauty to match any romantic tropical destination.

212-213 • The Scala dei
Turchi (Turks' Staircase),
near Agrigento, is an
impressive and picturesque
marlstone wall. Marl is
a sedimentary rock,
snow-white in color.

214-215 • The beauty of Cala San Felice, on the promontory of Gargano, is best described in terms of its three most precious jewels: rock, sea, and luxuriant vegetation.

215 • Tiny in terms of size but immensely enchanting, Cala della Pergola is one of the unquestionable marvels of the Apulian coast.

216-217 • Crepaccio is the smallest island of the Tremiti islands. At the bottom, is the somewhat larger San Nicola.

217 • San Domino Island is one of the largest of the Tremiti islands, as well as the most verdant.

● The Apulian coast near
Vieste delights visitors with
its beautiful beaches and
crystal clear sea.

220-221 • The Stacks of Torre dell'Orso, in Salento, are called "the two sisters" due to the legend of two beautiful girls said to have drowned at this spot.

222-223 • The Gargano promontory is the spur of Italy. Surrounded by the Adriatic, its extraordinary coasts and beaches have been very popular tourist destinations for many years.

One STEP from HEAVEN

• Mont Blanc is the indisputable king of the Alps, as well as the most beautiful mountain in Italy.

INTRODUCTION One step from heaven

In ITALY, MOUNTAINS ARE MANY THINGS. THEY ARE FIRST AND FOREMOST A BIG PRESENCE: MOUNTAINS COVER MORE THAN 35 PERCENT OF THE COUNTRY. THE COUNTRY'S MAIN MOUNTAIN CHAINS ARE THE ALPS (INCLUDING OF COURSE MONT BLANC, MONTE ROSA, CERVINO, AND GRAN PARADISO), AND THE APENNINES (INCLUDING THE GRAN SASSO WITH ITS WORLD FAMOUS UNDERGROUND PARTICLE PHYSICS AND NUCLEAR ASTROPHYSICS LABORATORIES, MAJELLA, TER-MINILLO, AND FUMAIOLO).

ITALIAN MOUNTAINS ARE ALSO AN AMAZEMENT, AS WAS EXPE-RIENCED BY TURIN GEOLOGIST FELICE GIORDANO, WHO, IN AU-GUST 1864 COMPLETED THE FIRST ASCENT OF MONT BLANC (THE ROOF OF EUROPE, IN THE GRAIAN ALPS) FROM THE ESPE-

- The Pale Mountains, in an extraordinary and richly diverse natural park, are the largest mountain group in the Dolomites.

INTRODUCTION One step from heaven

CIALLY PRECIPITOUS ITALIAN SIDE, AND COULD GAZE OVER BREATHTAKING VISTAS AND FEEL THE INTENSE PRIDE OF SOMEONE WHO HAD CONQUERED A SUMMIT FOR THE FIRST TIME.

THEY ARE METAMORPHOSIS: LIKE THE IRIDESCENT COLORATION OF THE PICTURESQUE DOLOMITES (THE SO-CALLED ALPENGLOW), TODAY A UNESCO WORLD HERITAGE SITE, WHICH HAS INSPIRED POETS, THINKERS, SCIENTISTS, PAINTERS AND ARTISTS OF EVERY TYPE.

MOUNTAINS ARE ALSO A VENUE FOR CHALLENGING THE BITTERNESS OF AN ICY NATURE: EVERY YEAR, MEN AND WOMEN MAKING EVER MORE DARING AND PERILOUS ASCENTS UP SHEER CLIFF FACES.

THEY ARE CONNECTION: THE LONG TUNNELS (RAILWAY AND ROAD) LIKE THOSE OF FREJUS, SAN BERNARDO, SEMPIONE

INTRODUCTION One step from heaven

AND MANY OTHERS, WERE HACKED FROM ROCK TO FORGE TRANSALPINE COMMUNICATIONS IN ERAS WHEN ONLY EAGLES SOARED IN THE SKIES.

THEY ARE DIVERSION: IN ADDITION TO VARIOUS WINTER SPORTS, COMPETITIONS AND FESTIVALS ARE HELD FOR INCREDIBLE ICE AND SNOW SCULPTURES THAT ENCHANT THOUSANDS OF VISITORS EVERY YEAR.

THEY ARE WILD NATURE: ITALY'S MOUNTAIN RESERVES NATURAL AREAS AND PARKS ARE PACKED WITH INCOMPARABLE FLORA AND FAUNA. THAT INCLUDES THE NATIONAL PARK OF ABRUZZO, LAZIO AND MOLISE, HOME TO 2000 SPECIES OF HIGHER PLANTS, INCLUDING MANY VARIETIES OF COLORFUL ORCHIDS AND 60 SPECIES OF MAMMALS (AMONG WHICH ARE THE MARSICAN BROWN BEAR AND THE ABRUZZO CHAMOIS, AS WELL AS WOLVES, LYNXES, AND ROES), 300 SPECIES OF BIRD

One step from heaven

Introduction

AND 40 REPTILES, AMPHIBIANS AND FISH. THEN THERE IS THE SPECTACULAR NATURE OF THE TUSCO-EMILIAN APENNINES AND NATIONAL PARK TRAVERSED BY THE OLD VIA FRANCIGENA. THEY ARE MARBLE: MOUNTAINS PROVIDED THE RAW MATERIAL FOR SCULPTURES BY ARTISTS SUCH AS MICHELANGELO. BUT ITALIAN MOUNTAINS ARE ALSO SHOCKING: VOLCANOES LIKE ETNA (SICILY), VESUVIUS (CAMPANIA), AND STROMBOLI (AEOLIAN ISLANDS), HAVE WROUGHT PATHS OF DEVASTATION THROUGHOUT HISTORY, YET ARE ALWAYS EVOCATIVE, AS REPRESENTED IN THE PAINTING *ERUPTION OF VESUVIUS* BY JOSEPH WRIGHT OF DERBY. IN ITALY, MOUNTAINS ARE ALL THESE THINGS AND MUCH MORE BESIDES, ALL WAITING TO BE DISCOVERED.

● Picturesque images of an eruption of Etna, with a river of incandescent lava flowing between the rocks.

● The Dent du Géant (Giant's Tooth) is a high peak of more than 13.123 ft (4000 m) in the Mont Blanc Massif, recognizable by its unmistakable rocky skyline.

234-235 • Over the years the summit of Mont Blanc 15.781 ft (4810 m) has represented an irresistible challenge for many brave climbers.

235 • The glaciers and valleys of Mont Blanc boast some breathtakingly beautiful views, as does the whole of the Graian Alps that surround it.

The Mont Blanc Massif, a group of majestic mountains in the Graian Alps, wend their way along the border between French Haute-Savoie and Valle d'Aosta.

● The lovely Val Ferret (Ferret Valley) is in Valle d'Aosta, east of the Mont Blanc Massif.

The Teodulo refuge nestles on the slopes of the Pennine Alps. Built in the 1920's and recently renovated, it offers a fantastic view of Cervino.

242-243 ● A couple of Alpine ibexes move among the snows of the Gran Paradiso.

243 ● The extraordinary cat in the photograph is a European lynx, a rare sight among the mountains of Valle d'Aosta.

244-245 ● The incredible position of the Capanna Regina Margherita refuge on Monte Rosa makes for spectacular panoramic views over the surrounding scenery.

246-247 • Situated on the summit of the Signalkuppe in Valsesia, the Capanna Regina Margherita refuge is also an important meteorological observatory. The photograph shows the climb up to it.

247 • The Monte Rosa Massif is the second Alpine mountain group and extends from Italy to Switzerland.

● The skiing district of
Sestiere is part of Via
Lattea, which with
about 200 pistes
extends in part to the
Cottian Alps.

250 • A majestic example of the Alpine ibex climbs with ease among the high rocks of the Gran Paradiso.

250-251 • Monviso in the Cottian Alps is nicknamed the "King of Stone". The River Po emerges from its foothills.

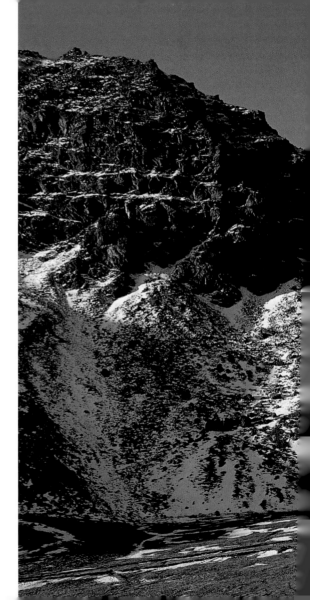

● Lo Stilfs offer skiing and the chance to come into contact with uncontaminated nature, protected by a national park.

The natural wonders
of the Valle di Braies
evoke the enchanted
scenery and
atmosphere of Alpine
legends.

● Close to the picturesque Lago Verde, the Lavarella refuge (in Alta Badia) is a true oasis of peace and beauty. In 2003 a chapel was built nearby.

258-259 • The Dolomites are famous for their gorgeous snowy views and the brilliant colors of the summits when the sun's rays bounce back off the rock.

259 • Alto Adige is a land of many marvels, of which Val Badia, near the Gadera river is one.

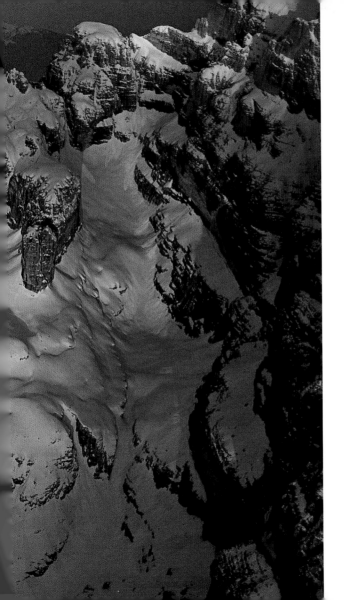

The Brenta group is
famous for its majestic
peaks bathed in the
strange light
of Alpenglow.

The Dolomites group called Sassolungo, whose main summit was climbed for the first time in 1869, marks the divide between Val Gardena and Val di Fassa.

264-265 • In 2009 UNESCO
declared the Dolomites a
World Heritage Site.

265 • Presanella (3558 m) is the
most important peak of the group
of the same name, in the southern
Rhaetian Alps.

● Since 1993 the Umbria-Marches Massif, covered by snow for most of the year, has belonged to the Sibillini Mountains National Park.

A breathtaking picture of the Gran Sasso, the Apennine sedimentary massif entirely within the borders of Abruzzo.

270-271 ● The Corno Grande (2912 m.), part of the Gran Sasso Massif, is host to the Calderone glacier, Europe's southernmost.

272-273 ●
The profile of Vesuvius, which covered Pompeii and Herculaneum with ash and lava in the famous eruption of AD 79, marks the horizon of the Gulf of Naples.

● Etna is one of the greatest marvels of Sicily: a mixture of extraordinary beauty, drama and the frightening power of nature.

A dense column of smoke rises from the crater of Etna, almost as if to remind the world of the volcano's fearsome power.

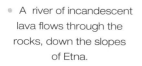 A river of incandescent lava flows through the rocks, down the slopes of Etna.

MINIATURE MASTERPIECES

- Alberobello's instantly recognizable small round stone houses, with their conical roofs, were declared a UNESCO World Heritage Site in 1996.

INTRODUCTION Miniature masterpieces

In *THE POLITICS*, ARISTOTLE SAYS THAT, "A GREAT CITY IS NOT TO BE CONFOUNDED WITH A POPULOUS ONE," A PROVERB THAT FITS ITALY'S SMALL TOWNS AND VILLAGES LIKE A GLOVE.

THE MARVELS OF ITALY'S LANDSCAPE MAKE PLACES, WHILE SMALL IN TERMS OF SIZE AND POPULATION, SEEM INFINITELY BIGGER. THE TOWNS AND VILLAGES OF ITALY ARE THE COUNTRY'S REAL JEWELS IN THE CROWN.

OFTEN FAMOUSLY BEAUTIFUL AND EXCLUSIVE TOURIST DESTINATIONS, THEY MAY BE ROCKY MOUNTAIN OR HILL VILLAGES, LITTLE TOWNS IN THE SUNNY COUNTRYSIDE HUMMING TO THE SOUND OF CRICKETS, OR SMALL SEA-

● One of the most picturesque villages in Italy, Vallo di Nera in Umbria looks like a typical medieval fortress surrounded by stone walls and towers.

SIDE RESORTS ALONG UNCONTAMINATED STRETCHES OF COASTLINE. WHATEVER THE SETTING, THEY ALL BEWITCH THEIR VISITORS WITH THEIR UNIQUE NATURAL AND MAN-MADE BEAUTY.

THIS IS CERTAINLY THE CASE WITH THE TINY BUT DELICIOUS PORTOFINO, WHICH GUY DE MAUPASSANT DESCRIBED AS "AN ARCH OF THE MOON," OR THE TOWNS OF LIGURIA'S FAMOUS CINQUE TERRE (MONTEROSSO, VERNAZZA, CORNIGLIA, MANAROLA, AND RIOMAGGIORE), OF THE COLORFUL VIPITENO, IMMERSED IN THE LUSCIOUS GREEN OF THE TRENTINO, NOT TO MENTION CAMPODIMELE, AN ANCIENT MEDIEVAL VILLAGE ON THE SLOPES OF THE AURUNCI MOUNTAINS KNOWN WORLD-

INTRODUCTION Miniature masterpieces

WIDE FOR THE SURPRISING LONGEVITY OF ITS INHABI-TANTS, OR SPERLONGA, WHERE, AFTER HAVING WALKED THROUGH THE WARREN OF ALLEYWAYS AT ITS HEART, WE SUDDENLY FIND OURSELVES LOOKING OUT ACROSS THE CRYSTALLINE AND GLISTENING WATERS OF THE TYRRHEN-IAN SEA.

WHILE WANDERING DOWN THE INNUMERABLE, WINDING ANCIENT ALLEYS OF THESE SMALL BUT FASCINATING LO-CALITIES, WE CAN SAVOR THE MYRIAD PERFUMES OF A CULINARY TRADITION THAT IS SIMPLE BUT UNRIVALLED, AS WELL AS THE WONDERS OF CRAFTSMANSHIP THAT CON-TINUES ITS TRADITIONS UNPERTURBED BY THE LATEST TECHNOLOGIES. WE HEAR THE SOUND OF JOYFUL DI-

Miniature masterpieces

Introduction

ALECTS SPOKEN BY PEOPLE LIVING AMONGST CLEAN AIR AND NATURE, WE WALK UNDER SNOW WHITE LAUNDRY FLAPPING IN THE WIND LIKE NATIONAL FLAGS, AND WE SEE OLD MEN WITH FLAT CAPS PULLED DOWN OVER THEIR EYES, SMILING AS THEY MEET.

FAR FROM ITS BIG CITIES, WE HAPPEN UPON INCOMPARA-BLE WONDERS IN EVERY NOOK AND CRANNY OF THIS FAS-CINATING COUNTRY.

- Set in the Monti Sibillini National Park, Castelluccio is 4921 ft (1500 m) above sea level.

288-289 • The lights of Cervinia, on the slopes of Monte Cervino, illuminate one of the most famous ski resorts in the Alps.

289 • A small sundial surmounts the bell tower of the church in Cervinia, dedicated to the Virgin Queen of Valle d'Aosta.

290-291 • The lovely tourist resorts on the bank of Lake Orta, in Piedmont, enhance its beauty and tourist appeal.

291 • The Benedictine Mater Ecclesiae convent is on the tiny island of San Giulio, in the center of Lake Orta.

292 • Malcesine is one of the most picturesque villages on the banks of the lovely Lake Garda.

293 • You can travel by boat from the marina of Malcesina to explore the coastline of Lake Garda, for many years a very popular tourist destination.

Trentino is a region abounding with typical mountain villages. The picture shows the center of the lovely Vipiteno.

296-297 • The atmosphere of Brunico, in Trentino, reflects both Italian and Austrian cultures, which have shared this land for centuries.

297 • The Piazza del Duomo in the heart of the city of Bressanone, the third largest in Trentino Alto Adige.

298-299 ● The curious nine pointed star layout of the town of Palmanova makes it a place of legendary charm.

300-301 ● A wonderful village overlooking a fantastic sea, Riomaggiore is one of the Cinque Terre of Liguria's Levante Riviera.

302 • The picture shows the warrenlike structure of Castel Vittorio, typical of many small villages.

302-303 • The medieval village of Castel Vittorio, in Imperia province, overlooks the picturesque Nervia Valley.

304 • The small fishing village of Camogli is famous for its multicolored houses mirrored in the Ligurian Sea.

305 • It's the beautiful little details of the villages that make them unique. This photograph shows a picturesque view of Camogli marina.

306-307 ◈ Fall in love with Liguria forever by paying a visit to the village of Laigueglia, whose every corner, viewpoint or square is a memorable discovery.

307 ◈ Portovenere is dominated by the imposing Torre Capitolare.

308-309 ◈ Portovenere is situated on a stretch of the Ligurian coast declared a UNESCO World Heritage Site in 1997.

310-311 ● San Gimignano, nicknamed the Manhattan of the Middle Ages due to medieval towers, is immersed in the green of the Tuscan countryside.

312-313 ● The town of Sorano, on the Tuscany-Lazio border, sits on a rocky crag nearly 1312 ft (400 m) high.

314-315 and 315 • Montepulciano, in the Province of Siena, is a tiny jewel of Etruscan origin, whose town center is still surrounded by medieval walls.

316-317 • The Tuscan town of Pitigliano strikes an enchanting balance between restrained urban development and the nature in which it is set.

The picturesque Clock Tower in the village of Brisighella, Emilia-Romagna, in the Faentino Apennine.

In winter snow blankets the plateau of Castelluccio in Umbria, while in spring it is covered by marvelous colorful flowers.

● Sperlonga, in Lazio, is delightful both during the lively summer season and in winter when it becomes a quiet village.

324 • Settefrati, a small village in the Province of Frosinone, looks down over the Comino Valley from a height of about 2625 ft (800 m).

325 • The medieval village of Latera is in the Province of Viterbo, close to Lake Bolsena and the Tuscan border.

● The amazing Island of Ischia
gives tourists great opportunities
for enjoyment away from the
beach, which however remains
one of its strong points.

Ventotene is the smallest inhabited island of the Pontine Islands off the Tyrrhenian coast. The island boasts a modern tourist port not far from a tufa rock, called Punta Eolo.

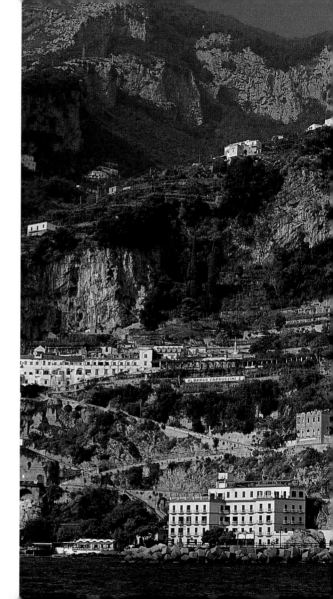

330-331 • The small town of Amalfi looks out onto the Gulf of Sorrento, whose lovely coast has been declared a UNESCO World Heritage Site.

332-333 •
he tiny village of Opi is immersed in the heart of the Abruzzo, Lazio and Molise National Park and is surrounded by spectacular natural beauty.

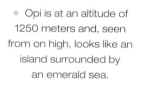 Opi is at an altitude of 1250 meters and, seen from on high, looks like an island surrounded by an emerald sea.

Alberobello is a small Apulian village known for its trulli, the famous dry white stone houses with conical roofs.

Vico del Gargano, a small village in the heart of the Gargano Promontory, becomes a popular tourist destination in summer. Its center is a tangle of alleyways redolent with the atmosphere of a distant era.

340-341 • The austere Romanesque Bitonto Cathedral is home to a splendid griffin floor mosaic.

341 • A detail of Bitonto Cathedral: one of the two stone griffins which support the arch of the central doorway.

342 • Picturesque Massafra castle in the Province of Taranto overlooks the ravine of San Marco.

343 • The town of Massafra is known for its many ravines, rocky corridors whose cavities have hosted human settlements through the ages.

344 • Walking through the alleyways of the Junno district in Monte Sant'Angelo, we taste the authenticity of a simple and traditional way of life.

344-345 • A picture of the Junno quarter of Monte Sant'Angelo, in Apulia. The houses packed close one against the other make them an even more distinctive sight.

346-347 ● Small and gorgeous places like the village of Bosa help us discover the beauty of authentic Sardinia.

348-349 ● The medieval village of Castelsardo looks out directly onto the Gulf of Asinara. Its unusual position makes for breathtaking views.

Linosa is a magnificent volcanic island in Sicily's Pelagie Islands archipelago. The pleasant colors of the houses act as a foil to the colorful natural scenery swathing the island.

CLEAR, COOL WATERS

- The Benedictine convent of Mater Ecclesiae on San Giulio Island
in Lake Orta was founded in 1973.

INTRODUCTION Clear, cool waters

Water is the cradle of life in Italy, and not just because the peninsula is surrounded by water. Its river system constitutes its arteries, its lifeblood, and the land is refreshed and made fertile by lakes dotted across its length and breadth. After wending its way across the Po Valley, the River Po, Italy's main river, fed by many tributaries, empties into the Adriatic. In doing so it creates an enchanting and varied landscape, a UNESCO World Heritage Site. The historic Piave is another northern river and the subject of one of the most famous Italian patriotic songs, *THE LEGEND OF THE PIAVE*, BY E.G. MARIO).

- The name of the Marmore Waterfalls, near Terni, derives from the calcium salts on the rocks that resemble marble.

INTRODUCTION Clear, cool waters

THE VALPADANA IS DOTTED WITH GORGEOUS LAKES: SUCH AS LAKE COMO, WHICH IS THE BACKDROP TO BIG VILLAS AND HISTORIC BUILDINGS SUCH AS VILLA D'ESTE, VILLA MONASTERO, VEZIO CASTLE, VILLA PLINIANA, THE VOLTIAN TEMPLE, AND VILLA CARLOTTA; LAKE MAGGIORE, SURROUNDED BY MOUNTAINS, GARDENS, CASTLES, MUSEUMS, MOUNTAINS, GARDENS, CASTLES, AND NATURAL PARKS; LAKE GARDA, THE LARGEST OF THE ITALIAN LAKES SET BETWEEN LOMBARDY, THE VENETO, AND TRENTINO ALTO-ADIGE; THE LAKE OF ISEO, WITH ITS YEAR-WIDE TOURISM, WATER SPORTS, FISHING AND MUSICAL EVENTS.

THE LEGENDARY TIBER RUNS THROUGH CENTRAL ITALY. MYTH HAS IT THAT IT WAS TO THESE WATERS THAT ROMULUS (FOUNDER AND FIRST KING OF ROME) AND HIS TWIN RE-

INTRODUCTION Clear, cool waters

MUS WERE ENTRUSTED, TO THEN BE SUCKLED BY A WOLF.

TUSCANY IS BLESSED BY THE MAGICAL PRESENCE OF THE ARNO THAT PASSES THROUGH A NUMBER OF CITIES, INCLUDING THE HEART OF FLORENCE WHERE IT SEEMS TO REDEFINE THE URBAN MASS AS IT MOVES LIKE AN INCREDIBLE FLUID WORK OF ART BETWEEN THE ARCHITECTURAL CREATIONS OF MAN.

THE CENTER OF THE PENINSULA IS CRISSCROSSED BY MANY RIVERS THAT MORE RESEMBLE BIG STREAMS, WHILE AGAIN IN THAT ZONE THERE ARE MANY LAKES, INCLUDING THE UNCONTAMINATED LAKE BOLSENA, SO GOOD FOR SWIMMING, THE TRASIMENO, THE FOURTH LARGEST ITALIAN LAKE, AND FINALLY LAKE BRACCIANO, WITH ITS ABUNDANCE OF FISH.

Clear, cool waters
Introduction

THERE AREN'T MANY RIVERS AND LAKES IN THE SOUTH AND ISLANDS BUT INSTEAD THERE ARE DYKES AND ARTIFICIAL LAKES. IN SICILY PEOPLE HAVE CREATED BASINS AROUND WHICH A HUGELY VARIED ECOSYSTEM HAS DEVELOPED.

AMONG THE INFINITE MARVELOUS LANDSCAPES OF ITALY, RIVERS AND LAKES ENRICH THE LANDS THEY BATHE, FILLING THEM WITH MAGIC AND CHARM AND EXCITING THE INTEREST OF PEOPLE WHO CANNOT RESIST THE CALL OF BEAUTY.

* The Po, a UNESCO World Heritage Site, is remarkably beautiful as it flows into the Adriatic.

360 ● Isola Bella, on Lake Maggiore, is home to the lovely Palazzo Borromeo, overflowing with precious works of art, as well as a spectacular Italian-style garden that wends its way over the lush terraces.

360-361 ● The tiny Island of San Giulio, right in the middle of Lake Orta.

362-363 ● Isola dei Pescatori (Fisherman's Island) on Lake Maggiore resembles a watercolor in the magical twilight.

362-363 • Menaggio, on the western bank of Lake Como, enjoys all the climatic and scenic advantages of its position between the lake and the mountains.

365 • Looking across from Menaggio we can enjoy some extraordinary views of romantic Lake Como.

366-367 ● The waters of Lake Garda, the largest of all the Italian lakes, lap against a number of towns in the provinces of Trento, Brescia and Verona.

367 ● Riva del Garda, in the Province of Trento, offers a bounty of culture, especially music, along with its wonderful views.

● Lake Garda is set between the Veneto, Lombardy and Trentino-Alto Adige and has been a magnet for domestic and foreign tourism for many years. Isola del Garda, with its neo-Gothic style villa and wonderful gardens, is one of the loveliest places in the area.

The rocky mountains of the Dolomites are reflected in the blue waters of Lake Landro, deep in the Val di Ladro valley.

372-373 and 373 • The magical atmosphere of the Fusine Lakes, near Tarvisio, bestow their beauty on the surrounding natural park.

374-375 • This aerial view shows the mouth of the Isonzo river (which feeds Slovenia and Friuli-Venezia Giulia), surrounded by a natural reserve of more than 5930 acres (2400 hectares).

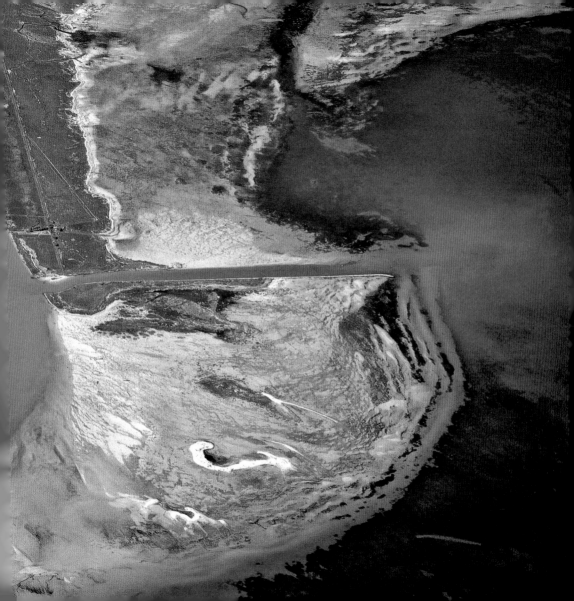

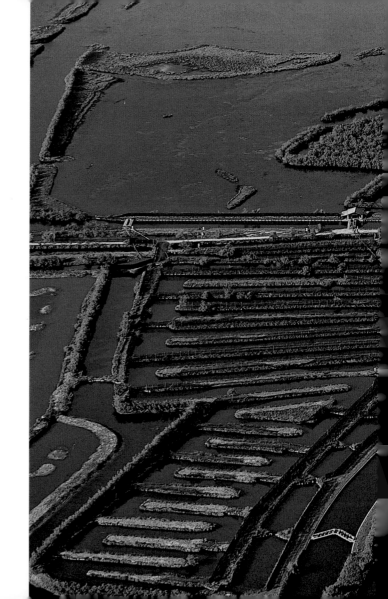

376-377 • After completing its long course, the Po river flows into the Adriatic via a complex system of branches that constitute the Po Delta. This photograph shows the network of canals in the Chioggia lagoon.

378-379 • The Po Delta contains landscapes of breathtaking beauty, such as the Po di Volano Nature Reserve.

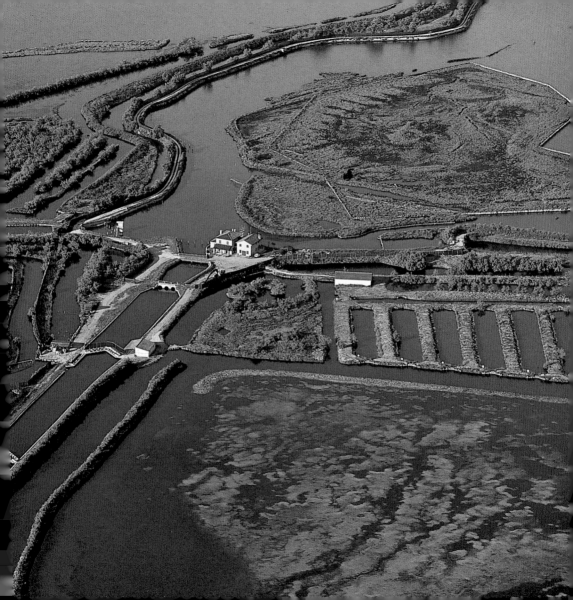

● The marshes near
Castiglione della
Pescaia are a protected
area with rich and
varied vegetation.

382 • On three levels, the Cascata delle Marmore (Marmore Waterfalls) envelops its surroundings in an amazingly beautiful cloud of water vapor.

382-383 • The near pristine natural environment of Lake Vico, near Viterbo, is an ideal habitat for the proliferation of extraordinary flora and fauna.

384-385 • Lake Trasimeno, tectonic in origin and quite shallow, is host to a particularly wide range of aquatic life.

386-387 • As well as being the most important river in central Italy, the Tiber is one of the jewels of Rome.

388-389 ● Lake Barrea, an artificial basin created in 1951, is one of the most picturesque tourist attractions in the National Park of Abruzzo.

390-391 ● The National Park of Sila, in Calabria, offers a great variety of views, including some lake.

392 • A view of Lake Cedrino, the artificial basin created by the damming of the Cedrino river near Oliena (Sardinia).

393 • The Tirso is Sardinia's main river, dammed to create an artificial basin. Indeed, the region has very few natural basins.

394-395 and 395 • The Alcantara is one of Sicily's main rivers, with natural gorges created by lava flows along its route.

396-397 • Trapani is known as the 'salt city ' because of its abundant salt-pans.

WONDERS
in GREEN

- The hills of Monferrato, in Piedmont, are known the world over for their extraordinary wines and spumanti.

INTRODUCTION Wonders in green

CLOAKED IN A GREEN AS INTENSE AND VIVID AS THAT OF THE NATIONAL FLAG, THE PLAINS AND HILLS OF ITALY COVER A LARGE PORTION OF THE COUNTRY'S LANDMASS, AND THE WINE AND AGRICULTURE OF THESE FERTILE REGIONS ARE FAMOUS AROUND THE WORLD.

THE PO VALLEY, PASSING THROUGH A NUMBER OF NORTHERN REGIONS, COMES IN MANY DIFFERENT GUISES, FROM THE PADDY FIELDS OF THE VERCELLI PLAIN, WHICH PROVIDED THE BACKGROUND TO THE NOBLE AND ENCHANTING BEAUTY OF SILVANA MANGANO IN THE FILM *RISO AMARO*; TO THE UNDULATING AND PARTIALLY WOODED STRETCHES OF LANGHE, ROERO AND MONFER-

● Tuscany is a very hilly region: from the Livorno to the Pisan hills, to those of Albenga, Fiora alle Metallifereand the hills of Chianti, famous for their wine.

INTRODUCTION Wonders in green

RATO; THE PO DELTA, WHOSE UNSPOILED NATURAL BEAU-
TY HAS MADE IT A UNESCO WORLD HERITAGE SITE; AND
THE VENETO, WHOSE BERICI AND EUGANEI HILLS ARE CON-
NECTED GEOLOGICALLY AS WELL AS GEOGRAPHICALLY.

AROUND PISA IN TUSCANY, A STRETCH OF THE VALDARNO
(THE FLOOD PLAIN NAMED AFTER THE ARNO RIVER) BOR-
DERS THE HILLY REGION OF CHIANTI, FAMOUS FOR ITS
WINE. THE MAREMMA PLAIN EXTENDS ALONG THE
TYRRHENIAN SEA, ITS SPLENDID BEACHES ALTERNATING
WITH DENSE PINE FORESTS, TINY COVES WASHED BY AN
ADAMANTINE SEA, NATURAL AREAS, PARKS, RESERVES,
ENCHANTING HAMLETS AND ANCIENT CASTLES. THE RO-
MAN CAMPAGNA EXTENDS ITS WAY AROUND THE CITY'S
HILLS. HERE, ALONG THE CONSULAR ROADS, WE FIND A

INTRODUCTION Wonders in green

MASS OF ARCHAEOLOGICAL ROUTES, LOCAL PRODUCTS AND A CENTURIES' OLD CULINARY TRADITION.

FURTHER SOUTH, FOOD CROPS GROW EASILY IN THE MILD CLIMATE OF THE PONTINE MARSHES, THE KIWI-PRODUCING REGION OF ITALY. VOLTURNO AND SELE ARE THE MAIN PLAINS IN CAMPANIA, VERY FERTILE AND THEREFORE DENSELY POPULATED, BUT THE TAVOLIERE DELLE PUGLIE IS THE BIGGEST PLAIN IN SOUTHERN ITALY, AND AN OLD MIGRATION ROUTE FOR SHEEP. EVEN FURTHER SOUTH, THE SALENTINE PLAIN SPRAWLS OVER A VAST FLAT EXPANSE. CALABRIA'S MAIN PLAINS ARE THE SIBARI AND THE GIOA TAURO. PALERMO IS IMMERSED IN THE GORGEOUS CONCA D'ORO (KNOWN FOR ITS MANDARINS), BUT THE CATANIA PLAIN IS THE LARGEST IN SICILY. IN SARDINIA, THE COUN-

Wonders in green
Introduction

TRYSIDE IS SYNONYMOUS WITH THE VAST CAMPIDANO PLAIN IN THE SOUTHWEST OF THE ISLAND, HOME TO PINK FLAMINGOS. IT IS NOT JUST VISITORS WHO ARE AMAZED AND STIRRED BY THE BEAUTIFUL COUNTRYSIDE AND HILLS OF ITALY. LOCALS, DESPITE THEIR FAMILIARITY WITH THE LAND, NEVER CEASE TO APPRECIATE THE WONDERS ON THEIR OWN DOORSTEP.

● Tuscany's lovely hilly areas frame the beauty of a region packed with art and history.

406-407 • The small town of La Morra is immersed in the countryside of the Langhe and surrounded by seven footpaths, all merging into the circular one of Barolo, source of the famous wine produced in the area.

408-409 • The Vercelli paddy-fields provided the setting for the movie *Riso Amaro (Bitter Rice)*, a neorealist masterpiece starring Silvana Mangano.

410-411 • An aerial view of the farming areas of Asti and Alessandria, in Piedmont.

Some views of the Cuneo countryside evoke a hint of the hazy atmosphere of Impressionist masterpieces.

In the hilly zones of the Oltrepò Pavese we find typical wineries with their extraordinary local wines.

● The countryside of
the Tuscan-Emilian
Apennines swathed
in a thick mist, which
accentuates
its charm.

418-419 ● Meldola, in Emilia-Romagna, is set in a lovely hilly area near the Bidente river, not far from Forlì.

419 ● The rural surroundings of Ferrara, the beautiful city of the Estensi family on the Emilian plain.

420-421 ● The marvelous pastel colors of the Sienese hills make for one of the most spectacular views in the whole of Tuscany.

421 ● The famous Balze di Volterra are the result of rainwater erosion.

422 and 422-423 ● The Viterbo countryside is as lovely as the city it surrounds, rich in history and prestigious monuments.

424-425 ● The incredibly picturesque natural landscape of the Castelluccio plain emerges in the heart of the Monti Sibillini National Park, between Umbria and the Marches.

● Flocks grazing in the
countryside between Norcia and
Gubbio. Visitors to Umbria can
relax in the midst of a lovely
bucolic setting.

428-429 • A thin mist envelopes Campotenese, a hamlet in the municipality of Morano Calabro.

430-431 • Motta Montecorvino is a tiny sub-Apennine jewel in the Province of Foffia. The photograph shows the picturesque landscape of the Monti Dauni.

● A group of trulli, characteristic dry white stone houses with conical roofs, in Ceglie Messapica, in the province of Brindisi.

434-435 • The olive trees that populate the Nardò countryside contribute to Apulia's excellent olive oil, among the finest in Italy.

435 • Vineyards and wine production are a fantastic source of wealth for the Valle dell'Ofanto (Offanto Valley), named after the main river in Apulia, which is also one of the most important in the South.

436-437 • The small town of Dorgali, in the Province of Nuoro, is one of the region's myriad treasures. The photograph shows a grazing flock.

437 • A beautiful picture of pastureland in Sardinia. The island is full of wonderful views.

438-439 • The Ragusa highland, teeming with abundant Mediterranean vegetation.

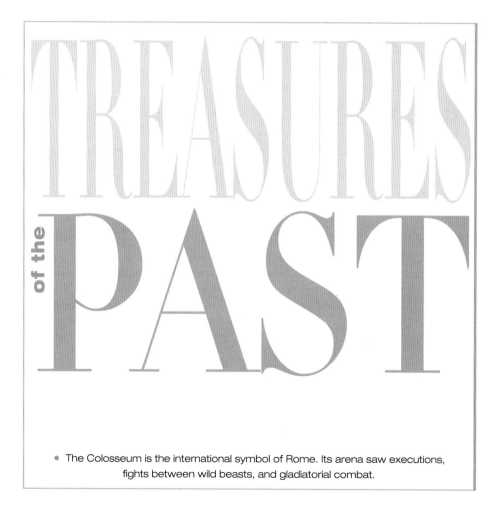

TREASURES
of the PAST

- The Colosseum is the international symbol of Rome. Its arena saw executions, fights between wild beasts, and gladiatorial combat.

INTRODUCTION Treasures of the past

ARCHITECTURALLY SPEAKING, ITALY IS A MOSAIC: THE ENTIRE PENINSULA IS STREWN WITH MAJOR SITES, MONUMENTS, BUILDINGS AND EXCAVATIONS WHICH, LIKE A SERIES OF PRECIOUS ENAMELED MOSAIC TILES DISCOVERED AND PIECED TOGETHER ONE BY ONE, SERVE TO GIVE US A CLEARER PICTURE OF THE PAST.

THESE SHARDS OF HISTORY RANGE FROM THE VERONA ARENA, AN ANCIENT ROMAN AMPHITHEATER IN THE HEART OF THE CITY, TO ANCIENT NECROPOLISES, LIKE THE ETRUSCAN TOMBS OF TARQUINIA AND CERVETERI (THE FAMOUS SARCOPHAGUS OF THE SPOUSES WAS DISCOVERED AT THE BANDITACCIA NECROPOLIS), TO THE CITIES OF HERCULANEUM AND POMPEII, BURIED AND CONSIGNED TO HISTORY BY THE

● A detail of one of the extraordinary frescoes decorating the House of the Golden Bracelet in Pompeii, on the intersection between the Via Consolare and Via delle Terme.

INTRODUCTION Treasures of the past

LAVA OF VESUVIUS IN 79 B.C. THEN THERE IS PAESTUM, AN ANCIENT TOWN IN MAGNA GRECIA SACRED TO POSEIDON, WHERE WE FIND THE EXTRAORDINARY REMAINS OF THE TEMPLES OF HERA, ATHENA, AND NEPTUNE. FROM THERE WE CAN TRAVEL TO THE VALLEY OF THE TEMPLES IN AGRI-GENTO, TODAY A UNESCO WORLD HERITAGE SITE, AND ALSO TO THE ANCIENT GREEK THEATERS OF SYRACUSE AND TAORMINA, WHERE WE CAN VIVIDLY FEEL THE LIVING PRES-ENCE OF HISTORY.

THE ARCHAEOLOGY OF ROME MERITS A SECTION ALL TO IT-SELF, AND NO ONE BOOK COULD CONTAIN IT ALL. PERHAPS MOST ICONIC IS THE MAJESTIC COLISEUM, STANDING PROUD AND DIGNIFIED, A BEACON OF ANCIENT CIVILIZATION AMIDST TODAY'S ENDLESS MERRY-GO-ROUND OF CARS, BUSES AND

SCOOTERS. THEN THERE IS THE FORUM, AT ONE TIME THE HEART OF THE PUBLIC AND POLITICAL LIFE IN THE CITY FOR OVER A MILLENNIUM. FINALLY LET'S NOT FORGET THE EARLIEST SETTLEMENT ON THE PALATINE HILL, AND THE MANY AND ATMOSPHERIC CHRISTIAN CATACOMBS DOTTING THE ROADS JUST OUTSIDE THE ANCIENT CITY.

MUSEUMS PERFORM A KEY ROLE IN THE PRESERVATION OF ITALY'S IMMENSE ARCHITECTURAL HERITAGE: AMONG THEM THE NATIONAL MUSEUM OF ROME (AT ITS PALAZZO MASSIMO SITE), WHICH HOUSES THE *LANCELLOTTI DISCOBOLUS* AND MUCH MORE; THE NATIONAL MUSEUM OF REGGIO CALABRIA WITH THE RIACE BRONZES, AN EXTRAORDINARY UNDERWATER ARCHAEOLOGICAL FIND; AND THE MUSEUM OF NAPLES, WITH ITS GREAT COLLECTION OF RELICS FROM DATING FROM

Treasures of the past
Introduction

PREHISTORY TO LATE ANTIQUITY. VERY FEW OTHER COUNTRIES CAN BOAST A CONCENTRATION OF ARCHAEOLOGICAL WEALTH EQUAL TO THAT OF ITALY. AND WITH ALL PROBABILITY THE EARTH STILL CONCEALS MANY MORE TREASURES THAN IT HAS YET TO YIELD UP.

TODAY, THANKS TO THE EFFORTS OF THE MUSEUMS, THIS HERITAGE IS ACCESSIBLE TO EVERYONE AND SEEN BY VISITORS FROM ALL OVER THE WORLD. THIS REALLY IS A VARIED AND COLORFUL MOSAIC, AN EXPRESSION OF WHAT WE CAN SAFELY CALL THE INFINITE MARVELS OF ITALY.

- Taormina's ancient greek theatre is situated in an extraordinarily panoramic position. From its steps you can admire both Etna and the Ionian Sea.

● Aquileia is home to the remains
of an extraordinary Roman Forum,
the ancient trading and meeting
area that represented the real
heart of the city.

450 • The 988 acres (400 hectares) of the necropolis at Cerveteri (Banditaccia) is one of the most magnificent and interesting Etruscan necropolises ever discovered.

450-451 • The necropolis of Banditaccia (declared a UNESCO World Heritage Site in 2004) houses, along with thousands of graves, the Tomb of the Reliefs, dating from the fourth century BC.

452-453 •
Emperor Hadrian built
his vast and fascinating
villa complex
near Rome.

454-455 •
At one end of the long
canal of Hadrian's Villa
we find the
nymphaeum dedicated
to Serapis. On the
opposite side we see
majestic statues and
columns.

456 • The Arch of Septimus Severus (third century AD), at the foot of the Capitoline, is an impressive monument that celebrates the military victories of Severus.

456-457 • The grandiose complex of Trajan's Forum, where formal public ceremonies were held, is home to the majestic Basilica Ulpia and Trajan's Column.

458-459 ● The remains of the Baths of Caracalla, an immense thermal complex dedicated to body care and sport.

460-461 ● A detail of Trajan's Column, an extraordinary monument celebrating the great military campaigns of the Emperor Trajan.

462-463 ● The atmosphere of the ancient Roman Forum catapults the visitor into a dimension steeped in history and timeless appeal.

464 • Ostia Antica's main thoroughfare passed a number of public buildings, including the theatre.

464-465 • At the intersection between the main axis and the cardo, we find the Capitolium, the main temple of Ostia Antica that dominates the ruins from on high.

● The wonderful
Roman theatre of Ostia
Antica is still the venue
for events and shows.

468 ● An aerial view of the amphitheatre at Pozzuoli. The building once held up to 20,000 spectators.

468-469 ● A picture of the arches of Pozzuoli. In ancient times the city was an important trading port, connected to Rome via a good road network.

470 • The house of Neptune and Amphitrite is one of the best-preserved sites in Herculaneum. The photograph shows a detail of a wall mosaic.

471 • The Jeweled House in Herculaneum is one of the extraordinary Roman residences that occupy the archaeological area of the city, buried under the lava of Vesuvius in AD 79.

472-473 •
Picturesque ruins of
the city of Pompeii,
destroyed by the
eruption of Vesuvius
in AD 79.

474-475 • Vesuvius
provides the
background for the
splendid Temple of
Jove in Pompeii, whose
ruins seem to challenge
the passage of time
with their unflustered
elegance and self-
assurance.

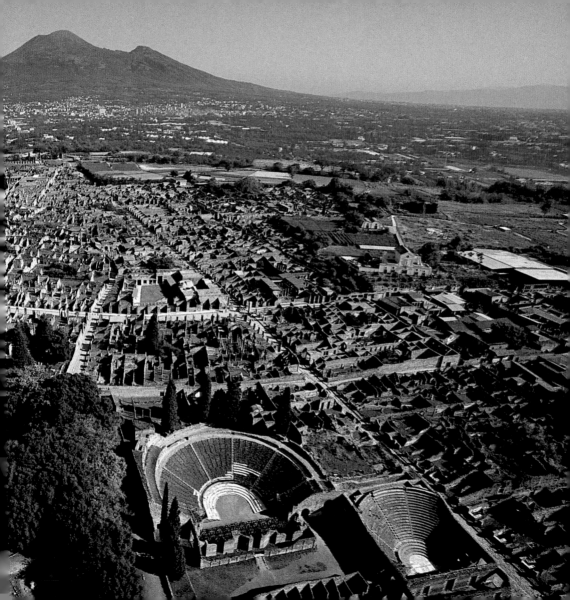

476 ● The Temple of Apollo was an important religious building in the heart of ancient Pompeii, situated in a sacred area surrounded by columns.

476-477 ● At certain times of the day, the play of shadows on the ruins along Via dell'Abbondanza in Pompeii seems to give new life to the buried city.

478 ● The luxurious entrance of the House of the Small Fountain left visitors with no doubts about the social class of its inhabitants.

479 ● The Tuscan atrium and the Tablinum of the house of Marcus Lucretius Frontonius in Pompeii, an elegant home in an excellent state of preservation.

480-481 ● The Villa of Mysteries, well known for its pictorial representation of the marriage of Bacchus and Ariadne, is another of Pompeii's priceless jewels.

The Nuraghe Santu
Ariadne, dating from
the Bronze Age,
is the hub of the
archaeological site
at Torralba, in Sardinia.

484 e 484-485 • The ancient Sicilian city of Segesta is brimming with archaeological marvels that fascinate the throngs of tourists who visit every year.

486-487 • The Greek theatre of Segesta is another of the breathtaking sights of the city founded by the Elymians.

488-489 ● The remains of the Temple of Heracles, in the Valley of the Temples, another area archaeologically fascinating area.

489 ● The Temple of Concordia is one of the extraordinary architectural masterpieces of the Valley of the Temples in Agrigento.

490-491 ● The Greek theatre in Syracuse has undergone a number of changes that nevertheless have left its irresistible charm intact.

The archaeological park of Selinunte is considered one of the main (as well as the largest) in Europe. The photograph shows Temple E, dedicated to Era.

The Greek theatre of Taormina is a magical place in which we can still sense the brooding presence of history.

INDEX

INDEX

INDEX

PHOTOGRAPHIC CREDITS

PHOTOGRAPHIC CREDITS

Pages 382-383 Giulio Veggi/Archivio White Star
Pages 384-385 Giulio Veggi/Archivio White Star
Pages 386-387 Antonio Attini/Archivio White Star
Pages 388-389 Luciano Ramires/Archivio White Star
Pages 390-391 Antonio Attini/Archivio White Star
Page 392 Giulio Veggi/Archivio White Star
Page 393 J. Ciganovic/De Agostini Picture Library
Pages 394-395 S. Montanari/De Agostini Picture Library
Page 395 F. Tanasi/De Agostini Picture Library
Page 396 Giulio Veggi/Archivio White Star
Page 399 Giulio Veggi/Archivio White Star
Page 401 Alfio Garozzo/Archivio White Star
Page 405 Giulio Veggi/Archivio White Star
Pages 406-407 Giulio Veggi/Archivio White Star
Pages 408-409 Marcello Bertinetti/Archivio White Star
Pages 410-411 Marcello Libra/Archivio White Star
Page 412 Marcello Libra/Archivio White Star
Page 413 Marcello Libra/Archivio White Sta
Page 414 Giulio Veggi/Archivio White Star
Pages 414-415 Giulio Veggi/Archivio White Star
Pages 416-417 Giulio Veggi/Archivio White Star
Pages 418-419 Giulio Veggi/Archivio White Star
Page 419 Giulio Veggi/Archivio White Star
Pages 420-421 Giulio Veggi/Archivio White Star
Page 421 Giulio Veggi/Archivio White Star
Page 422 Antonio Attini/Archivio White Star
Pages 422-423 Antonio Attini/Archivio White Star
Pages 424-425 Giulio Veggi/Archivio White Star
Pages 426-427 Giulio Veggi/Archivio White Star
Page 427 Giulio Veggi/Archivio White Star
Pages 428-429 S. Vannini/De Agostini Picture Library
Pages 430-431 Alfio Garozzo/Archivio White Star
Pages 432-433 Alfio Garozzo/Archivio White Star

Pages 434-435 Alfio Garozzo/Archivio White Star
Page 435 Alfio Garozzo/Archivio White Star
Pages 436-437 Giulio Veggi/Archivio White Star
Page 437 Giulio Veggi/Archivio White Star
Pages 438-439 Antonio Attini/Archivio White Star
Page 440 Marcello Bertinetti/Archivio White Star
Page 443 Araldo De Luca/Archivio White Star
Page 447 Antonio Attini/Archivio White Star
Pages 448-449 Antonio Attini/Archivio White Star
Page 449 Antonio Attini/Archivio White Star
Page 450 G. Carfagna/De Agostini Picture Library
Pages 450-451 S. Vannini/De Agostini Picture Library
Pages 452-453 Marcello Bertinetti/Archivio White Star
Pages 454-455 Antonio Attini/Archivio White Star
Page 456 Giulio Veggi/Archivio White Star
Pages 456-457 Massimo Borchi/Archivio White Star
Page 458 Marcello Bertinetti/Archivio White Star
Pages 460-461 Massimo Borchi/Archivio White Star
Pages 462-463 Marcello Bertinetti/Archivio White Star
Page 464 Giulio Veggi/Archivio White Star
Pages 464-465 Antonio Attini/Archivio White Star
Pages 466-467 Antonio Attini/Archivio White Star
Page 468 Giulio Veggi/Archivio White Star
Pages 468-469 Anne Conway/Archivio White Star
Page 470 Livio Bourbon/Archivio White Star
Page 471 Livio Bourbon/Archivio White Star
Pages 472-473 Antonio Attini/Archivio White Star
Pages 474-475 Antonio Attini/Archivio White Star
Page 476 Giulio Veggi/Archivio White Star
Pages 476-477 Giulio Veggi/Archivio White Star
Page 478 Araldo De Luca/Archivio White Star
Page 479 Araldo De Luca/Archivio White Star
Pages 480-481 Araldo De Luca/Archivio White Star

Pages 482-483 Giulio Veggi/Archivio White Star
Page 484 Giulio Veggi/Archivio White Star
Pages 484-485 Giulio Veggi/Archivio White Star
Pages 486-487 Giulio Veggi/Archivio White Star
Pages 488-489 Alfio Garozzo/Archivio White Star
Page 489 Marcello Bertinetti/Archivio White Star
Pages 490-491 Marcello Bertinetti/Archivio White Star
Page 492 Livio Bourbon/Archivio White Star
Pages 492-493 Giulio Veggi/Archivio White Star
Pages 494-495 Giulio Veggi/Archivio White Star
Page 504 Giulio Veggi/Archivio White Star

Cover, from left
first rank: Antonio Attini/Archivio White Star,
  Marcello Bertinetti/Archivio White Star,
  Antonio Attini/Archivio White Star
second rank: Marcello Bertinetti/Archivio White Star,
  Giulio Veggi/Archivio White Star,
  Giulio Veggi/Archivio White Star
third rank: Marcello Bertinetti/Archivio White Star,
  Giulio Veggi/Archivio White Star,
  Marcello Bertinetti/Archivio White Star
Back cover, from left
first rank: Marcello Bertinetti/Archivio White Star,
  Giulio Veggi/Archivio White Star, Marcello
  Bertinetti/Archivio White Star
second rank: Giulio Veggi/Archivio White Star,
  Alfio Garozzo/Archivio White Star, Marcello
  Bertinetti/Archivio White Star
third rank: Giulio Veggi/Archivio White Star,
  Antonio Attini/Archivio White Star,
  Massimo Borchi/Archivio White Star

Gabriele Atripaldi has a classical education and a law degree and has always been irresistibly attracted to words, to the point of making them his livelihood. He is fluent in English and has worked as an interpreter with many internationally famous writers. He has also translated a range of works for important publishing houses (biographies, technical works, comic-strips etc.) as well as for prominent magazines like *GQ* and *Rolling Stone* (for the latter, in particular, he had translated an exclusive interview with Obama at the time of his election, previewed in *Corriere della Sera*). A lover of writing in all its forms (from stories to song lyrics) he has been called a "narragista", that is, a narrator-editor, due to his remarkably cinematographic literary style.